Palm Springs

A California Desert Town

Written by Jane Centofante

Illustrated by Mike West

Boardwalk Press
Manhattan Beach 2017

Palm Springs

A California Desert Town

First Edition

BOARD WALK PRESS MANHATTAN BEACH

Text ©2017 by Jane Centofante
Artwork ©2017 by Mike West

Library of Congress Control Number 2017900186
ISBN 978-0-692-82355-2
Published by Boardwalk Press Inc.
Printed in China
boardwalkpress.com

10 9 8 7 6 5 4 3 2 1

Book design: Linda Warren, Studio Deluxe

"The great desert spa of Palm Springs is manifesting every symptom of becoming the playground of the world."

– *PALM SPRINGS LIFE* (1958)

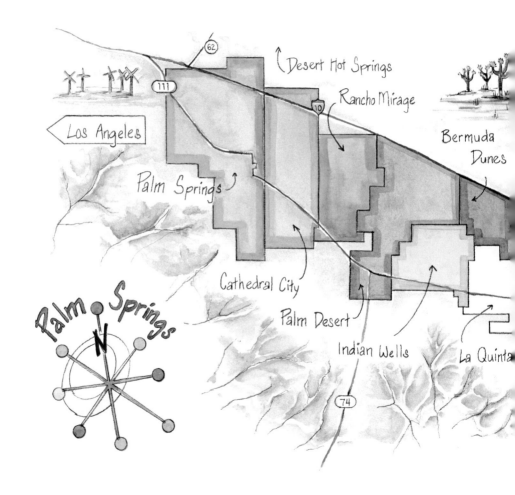

Desert Hot Springs

Rancho Mirage

Bermuda Dunes

Los Angeles

Palm Springs

Cathedral City

Palm Desert

Indian Wells

La Quinta

Palm Springs

N

62

111

10

74

Just the name "Palm Springs" conjures up images of a sunny playground filled with shimmering swimming pools, endless green golf courses and cool cocktails. But below this pleasure-seeking surface, is a town that has been reimagined countless times over the decades. Originally home to the native Agua Caliente Indians, "the Springs" attracted hearty pioneers in the early 20th century, eager to take on the challenges of harsh desert life in search of life-altering water. But before long, mid-century travel brought a new kind of seeker: one with a modern vision to turn an arid landscape into an oasis of fun and frolic. Movie stars arrived from Hollywood for rest and respite, while Midwest "snow birds" flocked to its warmer climes. Locals just considered it a happy haven. Today, Palm Springs and its surrounding towns have blossomed like vibrant cactus flowers, set against the backdrop of enduring desert sand dunes and majestic mountains reflecting the brilliant hues of a sunrise and sunset. An oasis turned paradise that still invites sun lovers to embrace the easygoing lifestyle — and relaxed attitude — of the Springs.

10

Phoenix

Indio

111

86

Salton Sea

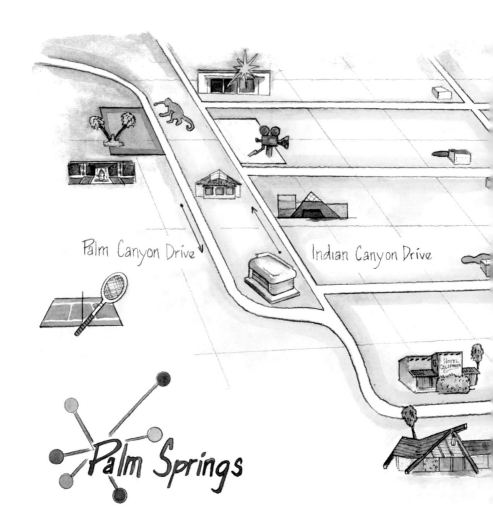

Palm Canyon Drive

Indian Canyon Drive

Palm Springs

Vista Chino

Tahquitz Canyon Way

Sunrise Way

Ramon Road

ACE

Whirling windmills wave a warm welcome
to locals and visitors alike

Coming or going,
it's easy spending along route 10

MORONGO

Dinosaurs and date shakes... enough to make anyone smile

Board a tram to snowy Mt. San Jacinto

after visiting a mid-century icon

Weekly pickings at a farmers market...

and three cheers for the Tour de Palm Springs

It's mid-century modern from the Uptown Design District to the Ace Hotel

Old Hollywood romped in the Movie Colony...

now new stars shine at the Palm Springs Film Festival

Fun and sun — past and present — at the Movie Colony Hotel

The 1946 Kaufmann House —

a stunning showcase
on the road to Modernism Week

PSP and the Palm Springs Air Museum... modern planes and vintage fliers

Before hipsters, Angels in the outfield hung their halos at the Parker

Favorite finds for foodies

Sonny loves Lucy along
the Walk of Stars

La Plaza — stairway to the Fabulous Follies of yesteryear

Art and architecture meet at the "Bob Hope house" and Museum of Art

Buzzin' around town with desert stars

Melvyn's

Copley's
ON PALM CANYON

Billy Reed's
LITTLE CLUB

Vintage watering holes
still serving up classic cocktails

The 1927 El Mirador and the
1959 Riviera wax nostalgic

Agua Caliente Indians and frontier pioneers
dwell on the Village Green

Indian Canyons

Murray Canyon

Palm Canyon

Hallowed hills of the Indian Canyons

Andreas Canyon

Tahquitz Canyon

Pride flags wave in the wind...

as a famous breeze catches Marilyn

Golfer's paradise

A silent-screen star's legacy and
fancy fountains light up Cathedral 'Cat' City

PICKFORD THEATRE

PICKFORD
THEATRE

NOW SHOWING!

The River flows in Rancho Mirage

View valley vistas from the Ritz...

then follow the pink brick rows to Sunnyland

Bob Hope leads by a nose in the annual Golf Cart Parade in Palm Desert

Life is theater at McCallum

and a vibrant Desert Street Fair

Jillian's and Keedy's —

from fine dining to counter culture

Birds and boats flock together at the JW Marriott

and furry friends gather at the Living Desert

Art and reflection inspire at La Quinta Arts Festival

Sentries stand guard at the 1926 "Queen of the Desert" at La Quinta Resort

Quintessential La Quinta: the Cliffhouse and St. Francis

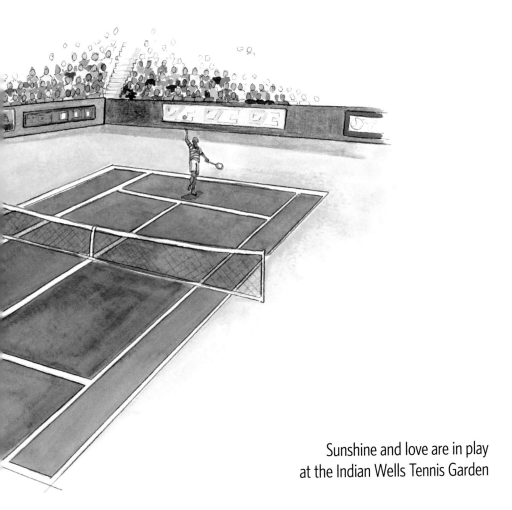

Sunshine and love are in play
at the Indian Wells Tennis Garden

A promenade of palms salute the Eisenhower Walk of Honor

Dine at Don Diego's...

Design at Karen Harlow's

Savor local specialities:
Murph's fried chicken and Shields' dates

85

Indio swings at Stagecoach...

and rocks for Coachella

Cabot's Pueblo and the Spa Zone are
definite destinations in Desert Hot Springs

The old West lives on in Pioneertown...

while the music plays on
at Pappy & Harriet's

29 Palms: proud Marines and creative artists
share a peaceful place in desert life

Eons and eccentrics have left their mark on the Salton Sea

With thanks

For both of us, this book would not have happened without the love and support of so many friends and family who keep us buoyed in both calm waters and stormy seas — and hot desert days. We gratefully offer heartfelt thanks to David Craddock, Linda Wenglikowski, and Michele Swanson-Wolcott, three for the road to Palm Springs; and our invaluable business manager Steve Smith, who keeps us laughing along the way.

Bringing this book to fruition was in large part due to the talents of more than a few gifted minds, especially Linda Warren and her talented colleagues at the Warren Group, whose collective eye for design is always beautifully expressed on the page.

We thank you all from the bottom of our hearts.

About the writer

Jane Centofante worked as a magazine editor before taking up life as a freelance editor of non-fiction books. She is the author of *Manhattan Beach: A California Beach Town* and *Santa Barbara: A California Coastal Town.* She and her husband share their time in Manhattan Beach and Palm Desert.

About the artist

Mike West is from just about everywhere but eventually settled in the Los Angeles area and attended the Art Center College of Design in Pasadena. He is the artist for *Santa Barbara: A California Coastal Town.*